TIPS FOR BETTER WRITING

LOUISE SPILSBURY

WAYLAND

First published in Great Britain in 2015 by Wayland

Copyright © Wayland, 2015

Dewey Number: 808'.042-dc23
ISBN: 978 0 7502 9103 3
Library ebook ISBN: 978 0 7502 9104 0
10 9 8 7 6 5 4 3 2 1

Wayland
An imprint of
Hachette Children's Group
Part of Hodder & Stoughton
Carmelite House
50 Victoria Embankment
London EC4Y 0DZ

An Hachette UK Company
www.hachette.co.uk

www.hachettechildrens.co.uk

Printed in China

Picture Acknowledgements:
Cover: Shutterstock: Jaren Jai Wicklund. Inside: Dreamstime: Olga
Bogatyrenko 29, Jmpaget 12, Randy Miramontez 22, Monkey Business Images
4, Redbaron 8; Shutterstock: Alhovik 17, Petrenko Andriy 23, Sebastian
Crocker 6, Vietrov Dmytro 27, Greg Epperson 24, Fluidworkshop 18, Mandy
Godbehear 25, Iaod 15, Juniart 14, Lisa S. 11, Michael Jung 1, Monkey
Business Images 5, 20, Xavier Gallego Morell 26, Pixsooz 19, John Michael
Evan Potter 13, Ivelin Radkov 7, Julija Sapic 10, Sunabesyou 28, Takayuki 9,
Merkushev Vasiliy 16, Jaren Jai Wicklund 21.

CONTENTS

HOW TO WRITE WELL

Do you want to explain why humpback whales migrate? Maybe you want to describe why you thought a film was really bad? Perhaps you want to write a short story about aliens and spaceships? Knowing how to write well helps you do these things and much more. Writing is an important part of a student's toolbox. It's fun, too!

A World of Writing

Different types of writing help you do different things. You can express your opinion in writing. This type of writing includes a writer's point of view. Reasons and facts support that point of view. A blog post can express an opinion. Another type of writing is information text, which clearly explains ideas and facts. This type of writing is used in school projects. A narrative tells of real and imagined events or experiences. It includes characters and details, and events happen in a certain order. For example, a story about your grandma is a type of narrative.

A library is a great place to explore different writing styles.

A computer is an important writing tool.

BASIC WRITING STEPS

TIPS FOR SUCCESS

You've found your topic and you know what kind of text you are going to write. Great, but don't start yet! To write well, you need to follow some basic steps to help you plan out what will fill your page. These are:

- **Research and take notes:** find out information about your topic and take notes.

- **Outline:** put your notes in order.

- **Write:** follow your outline to write your text.

- **Review and rework:** read your text. Show it to others. Think about how you can improve your writing. Rework your text.

Get Connected

Writing well takes some time. It's an important skill to learn, however, and the end result is great. Others will read your writing and your thoughts and ideas can connect you with the world.

CHAPTER TWO

WRITING OPINION PIECES

Good pieces of opinion writing come from strong feelings. If you can choose a topic for an opinion piece, choose something you feel strongly about. Do you think schools give pupils too much or too little homework? Do you think parents should give children pocket money or should they have to earn it?

Find Your Voice

Being interested in a topic affects writing in several ways:

Thesauruses, dictionaries and other reference books help you to use words creatively when writing.

- Your author 'voice' is your individual writing style. It's what makes your writing different from that of anyone else. Your writing voice is created by your choice of words and the tone of your writing piece, such as how serious it is. The more you care about your piece, the stronger your voice will be.

- When you care more about the subject of your piece, you'll put more effort into writing it and it will read well.

- If you care about the topic, you'll enjoy writing the piece more, too.

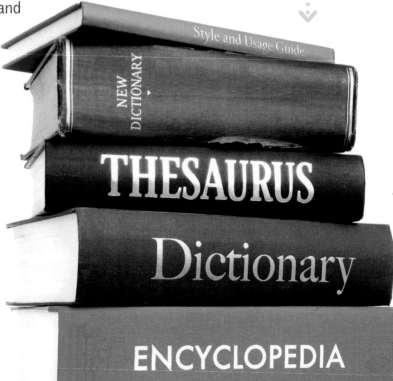

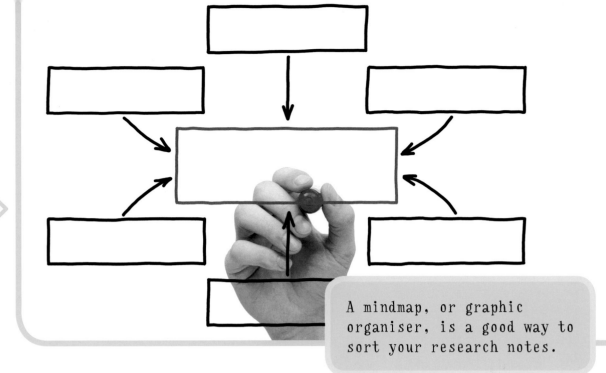

A mindmap, or graphic organiser, is a good way to sort your research notes.

Support Your Opinions

You need to be able to back up your opinions with facts and evidence. This requires research. You can research facts from websites, library books, encyclopaedias, newspapers and magazines. You can also use your local world for research, such as interviewing local people and friends.

Make a Note of it

Make notes about the facts you find. You could write down key words to remind you of your fact, or write a shorter version of the information you discover. For every opinion you give, you should have at least one example or some factual proof to support your opinion.

CHOOSE WISELY

Some sources are more reliable than others. Most reference books are good choices because they have been edited and then selected by a librarian. However, anyone can put up a website! Try to choose websites ending in .edu, .gov or .org because they will have been created by reliable sources such as universities or government departments.

TIPS FOR SUCCESS

WRITING AN INTRODUCTION

Once you have completed your research you can begin to think about writing an introduction. The introduction is the first paragraph of your written piece, and it's important for all types of writing.

The Importance of Introductions

An introduction tells readers briefly what the piece is all about. It usually includes a short summary of the issue. The aim of a good introduction is to:

- Map out what a reader can expect from your piece.
- Inform the reader about your point of view.
- Make the reader interested in reading more.

End With an Introduction?

Some people write the main part of the text and the conclusion before they write the introduction. This may sound odd, but the introduction should tell the reader what the piece is about and sometimes this is easier to do after writing the whole piece.

> Introductions count - you wouldn't introduce your friends without explaining who they are!

Interesting Introductions

An introduction should catch your readers' interest and make them want to read on. Many authors use one of three ways to make an introduction exciting:

- An anecdote: this is a very short story, often a personal one.

- A fact or a quote: this should be relevant to the topic, but intriguing or amazing. Ideally it should be sourced from an expert on the subject you are writing about.

- A rhetorical question: a question to which you don't expect an answer. Again, it should grab the reader's attention, such as 'Are you willing to watch polar bears die of starvation?'

Great introductions keep your readers interested!

TIPS FOR SUCCESS

SETTING THE TONE

Your introduction should set the tone for the rest of the piece, too. A serious subject, such as pollution, requires formal, serious language — even in any personal anecdotes you might use. However, if you're writing about why you dislike school trips, you might use an informal tone and use jokes to make your writing funny.

PLANNING OPINION PIECES

Now you have some facts to support your opinions and a great introduction – what next? The next step is to organise your piece. Before you write the main body of any piece of writing it is essential to have a plan. Having a plan ensures a piece is interesting but also flows in an easy-to-follow way. A plan also makes writing a piece a lot easier!

What, Why and How?

In an opinion piece, you'll probably have several reasons to back up your opinions. Most people start with their weakest argument and end with their strongest. Plan to cover one idea at a time, like this:

1. What do you think?
2. Why do you think that?
3. How do you know?

By following this plan, first you give your opinion, then you give the reason for it and finally you give examples or facts to back up the reason.

Provide facts to support your opinions.

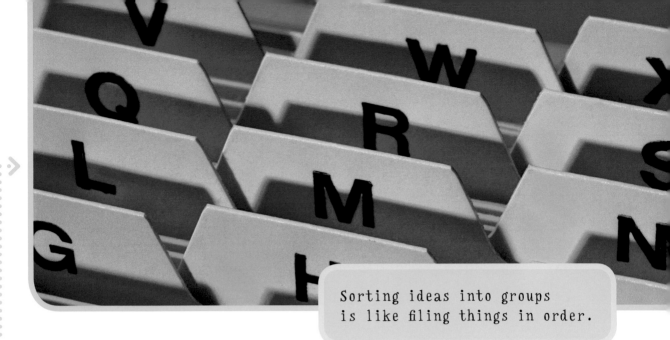

> Sorting ideas into groups
> is like filing things in order.

Make it Flow

Of course, it would be a little dull to write three separate sentences, such as: 'Cats are the best pets. They are more independent. My cat doesn't need walking. Dogs need walking a lot.' That's why writers use 'transition' words to make the text flow from one idea to the next, like links in a chain. So, you could say: 'I think cats make the best pets, because they are more independent. For example, my cat doesn't need walking. On the other hand, dogs need walking a lot!'

TIPS FOR SUCCESS

LINKS IN A CHAIN

Here are some transition words you could use to make your writing flow:

- **To introduce similar ideas use:** *additionally, besides, so, too, also, likewise, as well as, another* or *finally.*
- **To introduce a different idea use:** *in contrast, on the other hand, yet, despite, still, other people say, but, although* or *however.*
- **To continue an idea use:** *as a result, consequently, so, it follows that, therefore* or *eventually.*

WRITING INFORMATION TEXTS

You can guess the purpose of information texts from their name. Yes, they inform or tell people things! The difference between an information text and an opinion piece is that information texts provide objective information. That means the author gives information without expressing his or her opinion about it.

Know Your Audience

You can start work on an information text in much the same way as you start on an opinion piece. First, you come up with a title (if you haven't already been given one), then you brainstorm ideas and then you research your information. A key difference with an information text is that you need to know who your audience is. Ask yourself questions such as: who is the text aimed at? How old are they? What does your audience need to know to understand and learn from your piece?

Sometimes your audience might be younger than you.

> How would you organise a book about lions?

Ask a Question

Why not use a question in the title of your information text, to catch your reader's interest? For example, 'Why should you eat fruit and vegetables?' or 'How do elephants care for their young?'

Sort it Out!

An information text should provide clear information about a subject. When you begin to write, think about the main ideas you want to cover in your text. What are the important things you want your audience to learn about your topic? Once you have the answers to these questions, you can organise the notes you made during your research into groups. For example, if you're writing about lions, you might group your notes about where lions live, what they eat and how they hunt separately. Grouping notes will help you organise your text later.

TIPS FOR SUCCESS

IT'S DOWN TO DETAILS

When you're researching your information, look out for interesting details. They will make your writing far more interesting to read. Tell your readers something new that they probably don't yet know. For example, if you're writing a science text about light, include the interesting detail that there is no such thing as moonlight because the moon reflects light from the sun!

ORGANISING INFORMATION

If you want your readers to get the most from your information text, it's important to organise it well. Think of it like organising a desk or cupboard. If you put all the pens, paper, paints, glues and equipment in separate drawers and label them, you'll always know where to find them. It helps to organise information texts clearly, too.

Headings and Paragraphs

Headings work in the same way as labels. They tell the reader what's in the next piece of text. Headings are usually short – around one to five words long – and they help the reader to find his or her way around the book. Under each heading you might have one or more paragraphs. A paragraph usually consists of several sentences about a single idea.

When you have a lot of information, you need to organise it!

BULLETED LISTS

If you want to include several short pieces of information, you can put them in a bulleted list. Here is an example of a bulleted list:

- Bulleted points can be short and snappy.
- Some bulleted points are complete sentences like this.

Making it Work

When you have organised your headings and planned what ideas to put into your paragraphs, it's time to think about how to write the text. There are a few useful points you should know about information text. An information text:

- Is usually written in the present tense, such as 'This is how it works.'
- Is normally written in the third person, such as 'Tigers are a type of cat.'
- Is sometimes written in the past tense, if it is an historical report, such as 'World War II began in 1939.'

You can organise your information electronically, too.

Compare and Contrast

Keep readers interested by comparing and contrasting things. This helps to describe things to your reader. If you compare two things you can explain how alike they are. If you contrast two things you can explain how they are different. For example, 'Lions and tigers both have sharp teeth' or 'A lion's roar is louder than a tiger's.'

ADDING ILLUSTRATIONS

When you choose an information book, do you pick one that has only words, or one that has words, pictures, diagrams and other visual aids? Visual elements such as illustrations, charts and maps help readers to understand information texts and make them a lot more fun to read!

Doing a Better Job

Illustrations and diagrams are not only interesting – they also express some types of information better than words alone. For example, you might choose to include a cutaway drawing of a volcano in an information piece about volcanic eruptions. In an information text about the water cycle you might include a diagram like the one below.

Pictures are a fun and quick way to inform your readers.

LOVE THE LABELS

Don't forget to add labels to name the different parts of a diagram or illustration. You can also add arrows to an illustration to show the order in which things happen, such as the sequence of events that make up the water cycle.

Labels help readers to understand pictures.

crust
lithosphere
asthenosphere
upper mantle
lower mantle
outer core
inner core

Types of Visual Aids

So, you know you want to add some visual aids to your information text, but there are so many different types to choose from! Here are some ideas and some suggestions:

- A table or chart is useful for comparing things, such as different animals or rocks.

- A timeline is a bar with dates on that show different events. It is useful in a historical report or biography.

- Line and bar graphs can show changes over time or compare statistics such as the populations of different countries.

- A pie chart quickly shows the different proportions of something, such as different food groups.

- Maps can show location information, such as where important events took place or where bananas are grown and sold.

CHOOSING WORDS CAREFULLY

When writing an information text, you should choose your words carefully. Remember, you are explaining facts so you need to use the correct words to describe technical or scientific information. This makes your text more interesting to read – and makes sure that the information you write is accurate, too!

Making Words Work

Have you ever wondered why most information books have some words highlighted in the text and explained in a glossary at the end? This is because information texts often use difficult or technical words to explain things. For example, in a text about volcanoes you might use words such as 'lava' and in a text about wind power you might use words such as 'turbines'. These may be difficult words but the topic cannot be explained without them, so don't be afraid to use them. The key is to be sure that you understand any words you use and can explain them in your text.

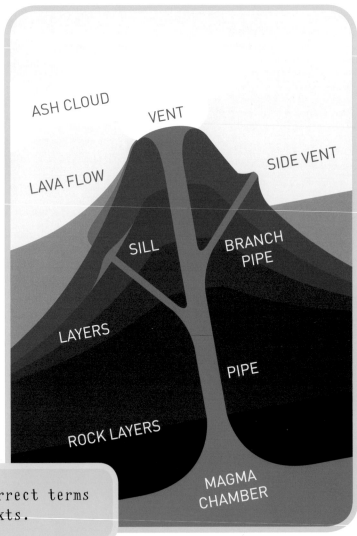

ASH CLOUD

VENT

SIDE VENT

LAVA FLOW

SILL

BRANCH PIPE

LAYERS

PIPE

ROCK LAYERS

MAGMA CHAMBER

Try to use the correct terms in information texts.

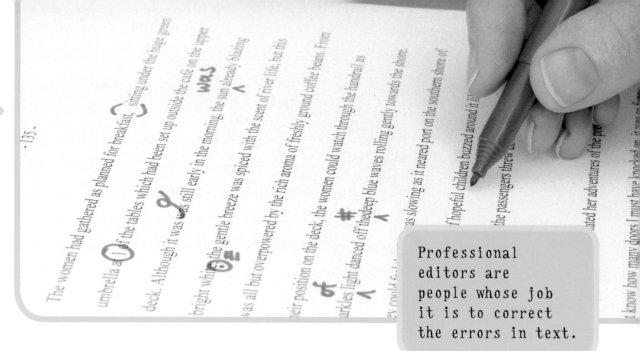

Professional editors are people whose job it is to correct the errors in text.

Editing Your Work

You will need to read through your text after writing it, to make sure it reads well. This is called editing. To edit all types of written work, you must read through it carefully and check for the following:

- Are all the words spelled correctly?
- Is the grammar and punctuation correct, such as having full stops and commas in the right places?
- Do the headings relate to what is in the text below them?
- Do you cover one idea in each new paragraph?
- Do all the paragraphs relate to the topic?
- Does everything make sense?

MAKE YOUR MARK

Even if you have already started using a computer to type up your work, it might be easier to print out a copy to edit. You can then mark any errors or areas you want to change in red pen.

TIPS FOR SUCCESS

CHAPTER FOUR

WRITING NARRATIVES

What is your favourite type of novel? Do you prefer detective stories, romances or comic novels? A narrative is a spoken or written account of connected events. There are many different types of narratives, so when writing a narrative your first job is to choose which type to write!

Types of Narrative

A narrative can be a fictional or true story. It can also be a combination of imaginary and factual events. Imaginary tales include mystery, romance, adventure, science fiction, fantasy stories, comic strips, myths, fairy tales, legends and fables. A factual or non-fiction narrative might describe an historical event or a recent incident from the news. A biography is a written account of another person's life, such as a famous politician or musician. An autobiography is a written account of a person's life, but one written by that person.

Some narratives are about real experiences.

Planning a Narrative

Even if you have a head full of exciting story ideas that you're eager to start writing about, it's best to plan your story first. Here are some things to think about:

- **Plot:** what is going to happen? What is the main thread of the story?
- **Setting:** where will the story take place? What time period is it set in – the past, present or future?
- **Characters:** who will the main characters be?

You could make a mindmap or a chart to note down some of these ideas for your narrative.

> Take time to think of and plan your narrative.

TAKE OFF!

Just as a good introduction is important for an information or an opinion piece, some strong opening lines are vital for a narrative, too. Look at a few of your favourite books to see how they begin. What do other authors do to get their readers' attention from the beginning?

TIPS FOR SUCCESS

NARRATORS AND CHARACTERS

Your next decision is who is going to tell the story.
There are three types of narrators and they each
tell the story in a different way:

• An All–Seeing Narrator:

This is not a character in the story,
but a person who knows what is
going on and is in all the characters'
minds. For example, *'Sam is playing
soccer in the playground, thinking
about his dinner. Jess is in class,
daydreaming about her party.'*

• A Third-Person Narrator:

This is when the author tells
the story from one character's
perspective. For example, *'Sam
thinks about what to have for
dinner as he kicks the ball, and
wonders what Jess is doing.'*

• First-Person Narrator:

This is when the narrator is
a character in the story – a
person who speaks for and about
themselves. For example, in Sam's
voice it would read, *'I think I'll have
pizza for dinner. I wonder where
Jess is now.'*

You can base a
character on
someone famous.

22

Creating Characters

So, you've decided on the narrator, but what about the other characters? How can you make them real? There are several ways to create characters with real personality.

- Decide how your characters look. Are they tall or short, blue- or brown-eyed? Do they have long or curly hair? What clothes do they wear? You could look at pictures in magazines for ideas.

- Base the character on someone you know, such as a friend, a family member or even a celebrity. This will help you describe how they look and react to things.

- Make them more human. Give good characters bad habits or weaknesses and give bad characters moments of goodness, too.

Make characters exciting but believable.

FILL A FILE

Create a file of facts about your characters, such as how old they are, who their friends are, who is in their family and what their hobbies are. Even if you don't actually use the facts in the story, it will help you imagine that the characters are real.

TIPS FOR SUCCESS

DIALOGUE AND DESCRIPTION

Imagine how meaningless a scene between two people would be if you didn't know what they were saying or where they were! Description and dialogue bring your characters to life and add interest to your narratives.

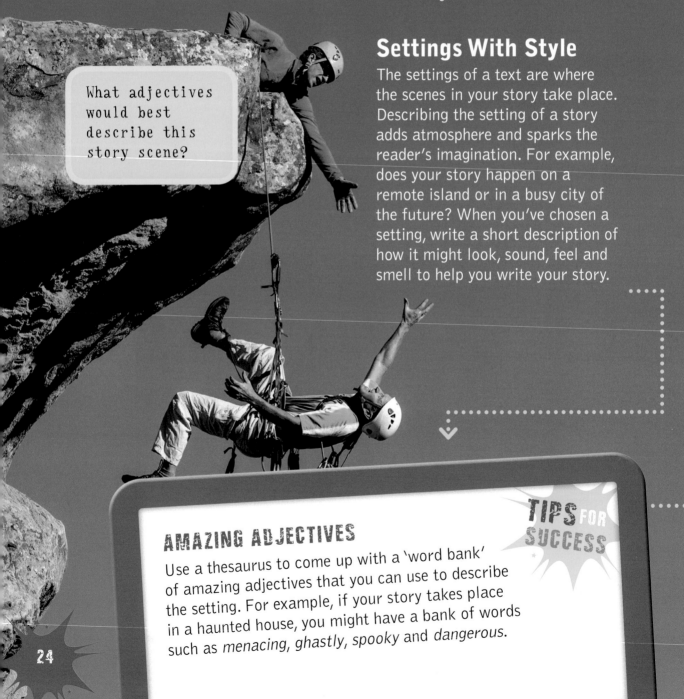

What adjectives would best describe this story scene?

Settings With Style

The settings of a text are where the scenes in your story take place. Describing the setting of a story adds atmosphere and sparks the reader's imagination. For example, does your story happen on a remote island or in a busy city of the future? When you've chosen a setting, write a short description of how it might look, sound, feel and smell to help you write your story.

AMAZING ADJECTIVES

Use a thesaurus to come up with a 'word bank' of amazing adjectives that you can use to describe the setting. For example, if your story takes place in a haunted house, you might have a bank of words such as *menacing*, *ghastly*, *spooky* and *dangerous*.

TIPS FOR SUCCESS

The Dialogue Deal

A conversation between two or more people in a narrative is dialogue. Dialogue reveals things about characters through their speech and their reactions to what other characters say. Dialogue also tells the reader important parts of the plot and helps bring scenes to life. Dialogue breaks up the text a little, too, because a new paragraph begins every time a new character speaks.

Talking Tips

- Never use dialogue instead of a description of an exciting event. For example, rather than a character saying, 'Look an avalanche!', instead describe the avalanche with exciting details and adjectives.

- Don't fill a conversation with long hellos, goodbyes or discussions about the weather! Try to skip quickly to the interesting parts.

Make it Real

Make your dialogue believable by using styles of speaking that fit the characters. For example, most grandmothers wouldn't say 'That's really cool!' Instead, they'd say 'That's lovely!'

Make dialogue realistic but dramatic, too.

25

MAKING NARRATIVES FLOW

What keeps you reading a story or a book for hours on end? Most good narratives build up a feeling of suspense, excitement or intrigue to keep the reader interested. This is sometimes called the 'narrative arc', which is really just a complicated way of saying that every story needs to have a beginning, middle and end!

Going Up and Down

An arc is like a hill. It goes up and then down again. This is how the action works in most narratives, too:

- In the beginning, the characters, setting and time of the story are set out. Events start to happen that build up to the middle of the story.

- In the middle of the story, the main character faces some type of problem or complication, and has his or her main adventures.

- At the end, any problems are solved and the complications are fixed.

Make your characters face exciting challenges.

26

A flowing narrative will keep a reader turning the pages!

Feel the Flow

Don't forget to use a variety of transition words and phrases to link the stages in your narrative and to help readers know when there is a shift from one time or setting to another.

Review and Revise

When you have written a first draft (a first attempt at your narrative), read it through carefully. Edit it, checking for spelling mistakes, punctuation and grammar. This is also your chance to make sure the story makes sense and flows well. For example, if the main character solves his or her problem using a particular skill, it might be good to show them using that skill early in the story. If one character seems a little unbelievable, you could add some dialogue or description to bring him or her to life.

TIPS FOR SUCCESS

READ IT OUT

One of the best ways to check that your story or narrative is flowing well is to read it out loud to yourself. You'll be surprised how much easier it can be to spot errors or places where part of a story is weak or missing when you read it out loud. You could also ask somebody else to read your story to you.

CHAPTER FIVE

HOW TO WRITE CONCLUSIONS

A conclusion is the part that ends or closes a piece of writing. Never underestimate the importance of a conclusion. It is the last thing your reader will read, so you want it to leave a lasting impression! Different types of text usually have different styles of conclusions.

Story Solutions

At the end of a narrative, try to end your story on a 'high' while also resolving the characters' problems. Some writers talk about what a character learned from their experiences. Some end with a 'twist' – a surprise that the readers could never guess! Perhaps you could write a 'cliffhanger' that hints that the character is about to go on a similar adventure?

Will you give your story a dramatic end?

Going Full Circle

Before writing your conclusion, re-read the whole text. Often an effective conclusion brings the reader full circle by tying together the beginning and the end. For example, a character might refer to a warning given at the beginning of a story.

TIPS FOR SUCCESS

Great writers always finish their piece with a great conclusion.

Other Endings

In an information text or opinion piece, the conclusion or last paragraph should not introduce any new information. The aim is to link your conclusion to the rest of your report and sum up what you've said before, without simply repeating yourself. Many people refer back to their introduction, and then show how they have explained the facts. They might also show how their examples have combined to support their opinion.

Ending Well

Remember, your conclusion is probably the main thing that your readers will remember about your text because it is the last thing that they read, so make it fantastic!

GLOSSARY

adjectives describing words. They tell us what something looks, feels, smells or tastes like.

brainstorm to try to solve a problem by thinking intensely about it

cliffhanger a chapter, page or narrative that ends in suspense

comparing describing the similarities or differences between things

complication an event, action or feeling that makes things difficult

contrasting describing the differences between things

cutaway drawing a picture in which part of the object looks like it has been cut away to reveal what's inside

evidence facts and information collected to support things we say

expressing saying, gesturing or writing what we mean

fables short stories that include a moral (show us the right way to behave)

fictional made up, not real

ghastly horrifying or shocking

legends stories about mythical or supernatural beings or events

menacing threatening

migrate to move from one place to another

myths old, traditional stories, often about gods and heroes

novel a long story or narrative

perspective a point of view

relate to connect to

sources books or documents used to provide evidence in research

suspense feeling of excitement and uncertainty about what is going to happen

technical based on precise facts

tense describes how verbs express time, such as past, present and future (is, was, will be)

tone a way of expressing oneself in writing

topic a subject or theme

underestimate to judge something to be less important than it really is

visual aids pictures, symbols, charts and diagrams that help to explain something that is written down or spoken

FOR MORE INFORMATION

BOOKS

CGP Books, *Key Stage 2 English The Study Book*,
Coordination Group Publications, 2012

Oxford Dictionaries, *Oxford Primary Grammar, Punctuation
and Spelling Dictionary*, Oxford University Press, 2013

Oxford Dictionaries, *Oxford School Dictionary*,
Oxford University Press, 2012

Thomson, Ruth, *It's Fun to Write Adventure Stories,*
Franklin Watts, 2011

OTHER 'THE STUDENT'S TOOLBOX' BOOKS

Royston, Angela, *Tips For Better Planning*, Wayland, 2015

Spilsbury, Louise, *Tips For Better Writing*, Wayland, 2015

Spilsbury, Louise, *Tips For Public Speaking*, Wayland, 2015

WEBSITES

For great tips and ideas about writing reports
visit the Writing Reports section at:
kidshealth.org/kid/homework/index.
    html?tracking=81347_I#cat20956

This website will help you construct and write
fabulous stories:
www.bookstart.org.uk/books/lets-write-a-story

You'll find lots of help with opinion pieces at:
http://teacher.scholastic.com/scholasticnews/magazines/
    scope/pdfs/SCOPE-011011-REPRO-19.pdf

INDEX